Financial Meatloaf

A Simple Recipe
For Financial Success

Cash Matthews

aBM

Financial Meatloaf

Published by:

A Book's Mind
PO Box 272847
Fort Collins, CO 80527

In Partnership with: Solomon Publishing

A Wholly Owned Subsidiary of Money University, LLC.

Copyright 2017 Cash Matthews
ISBN: 978-1-944255-35-0

Printed In The U.S.A. On Regular Paper. God Bless America And Her People.

Table of Contents

Chapter 1: Why You Will Love This Book.   1

Chapter 2: Why Are We Failing? It ISN'T ALL YOUR FAULT!   5

Chapter 3: Do Numbers Make You NUMB?   15

Chapter 4: Family Habits: Behavior Matters.
            Oh, And Your Kids Are Watching.   17

Chapter 5: Getting Started NOW Is So Easy. Feel better today!   21

Chapter 6: Safeguarding Your Family:
            There ARE Monsters Under The Bed!   23

Chapter 7: Getting Out Of Debt: G.O.O.D.
            (AND HOW TO STAY OUT OF DEBT FOREVER!) 25

Chapter 8: Quick Guide For The Self Employed.   29

Chapter 9: Take The Next Step. Now or never.   35

Chapter 1:
Why You Will Love This Book

Being broke sucks.

Mark Twain once said that you could learn to like a hot stove if you sit on it long enough. Most of the people that I have met in my lifetime are broke. I didn't say they were poor, I said broke. How can it be that in the richest, most educated country in the history of mankind, that most of the citizens in the United States are not doing well financially? For many, this is just the way it is and there is no obvious way out.

Perhaps you are reading this because you are sick and tired of being sick and tired? Are you ready to make some changes? As you look back over your previous years financially, how does that make you feel? Just so you know, you are not alone! The majority of Americans live bleak financial lifestyles during their working years and then again during retirement. In fact, many people retire on 30% of what they couldn't live on ALL OF the first time around! Is that you? Here are a few questions that might illuminate the situation:

1. If you had to retire today on all of the money you have saved up, how long could you survive?

2. Add up all of the money you've made over the course of your lifetime. How much of it do you have left?

3. Who taught you all about money? No offense intended, but was that person's life worthy of being copied, at least from a financial standpoint?

4. Are you ready to get started taking the right steps AND making the right changes?

5. Close your eyes for a moment and imagine how you might feel if your debt was paid off; if you had more money left over at the end of the month than your bills required; if you felt confident about your financial future, and if you were certain that everything was going to be okay. What would that be like for you?

Depending on how you answered question number four, it is time, right now, to get started!

The Statistics

I hate politics. At the end of the day you probably hate politics also. I can't find ANY evidence that tells me that our political system has really improved the daily walk of life for the average family. Yet every four years we divide camps, argue with our friends, and pretend to like one candidate over the other. We take sides and become divided among ourselves. Our strength as a group diminishes.

The problem is the system.

The answer is also the system.

Unfortunately the majority of Americans are headed toward an uncertain financial future. They have not taken care of their own health. They have not saved enough of their own hard earned money.

Now, we find ourselves in a position where they need someone else to pick up the slack. And this seems to repeat as an endless cycle of family financial mess.

What is the system? To me the system is an environment where each individual is free to choose their own route to life, liberty, and happiness! Usually, accomplishing these great things requires a MUCH from each individual. It requires all of us to get better, get more educated, gain knowledge from life not from just books, and to move up the financial food chain of life!

In America we have abundant opportunities for education. Past the age of 18 we have numerous colleges, trade schools, and technical schools. Entrepreneurship is on the rise in America as well. In fact the opportunity for almost everybody is abundant. Unfortunately, few people know how to operate the system. We simply don't know how to order from this menu of American Dreams.

Imagine for a moment you go into a room with your two-year-old child and on the table is a brand-new desktop computer still in the box. Let's assume that inside the box is the most wonderful, high tech machine available in the world today and is capable of doing wonderful things. Now, imagine that you brought your child to this room every day, eight hours per day for one year and never told them what was inside the box or how it worked. How might that turnout?

It is doubtful that the two-year-old would have opened the box, put the computer together, plugged it in, and then learned basic computing skills. There is nothing wrong with the computer system in this case. There is a lack of knowledge, understanding and perhaps a lack of desire on the part of the two-year-old. If you do the same exercise with a 15-year-old you might get a very different result! A normal kid today may have unpacked the computer, turned it on, set up a chat room and gone into an international online business all in the course of 30 minutes!!

The difference? Knowledge and Desire. One day, the two-year-old will have a deeper understanding of what is inside the box. One day the two-year-old will be a better driver of the machinery. And of course, one day the two-year-old will be 13 years old and will most likely be well-versed in how the system works

When it comes to money and finance do you know what's inside the box? Do you know how to operate the machinery? Or is it possible your money didn't come with a set of instructions?

Here are some numbers that absolutely freaked me out:

- **75%** of American citizens age 65 and above will live near the **poverty** line the **rest of their lives**
- The average 54-year-old person has less than $50,000 saved, plus a great amount of debt
- According to a recent survey, 55% of adults in this country could NOT come up with a measly $400 in the event of an emergency!
- Here is a scary number for some…if YOU had to retire today on the amount of money you have saved, how long could you survive? This is the most telling of all the statistics in the world…. your own number!

Chapter 2:
Why We Are Failing?

This chapter could be an entire book unto itself. Why are we failing?

First, there is this idea that everything is gonna be ok. There is this sort of mantra that floats around stating that everything works out in the end and we all get a happy ending at the end of our financial lives.

IT IS A LIE!

For most, the so called American Dream has morphed into the American Nightmare, and the shame of it all has kept most citizens from really reaching out, speaking up, and seeking the right kind of help. It is sort of like that old story about the guy who jumps off of a 30 story building, and exactly half way down, someone yells out, "Hey, how's it going?" To which the jumper replies, "so far so good!". See, jumping off of a building doesn't actually kill you. It is the harsh landing at the end that is so damaging. The harsh landing for most families is retirement and many of the issues that we face as we age.

For most, it is NOT turning out ok. I do not offer any of this as a criticism, rather a harsh look in the mirror to evaluate if your hard work has produced the right kind of fruit to feed you for the years to come. So, do this little test here real quick. We call it the Vomit Test"…..

The Vomit Test

1. How many years have you worked? _____ years

2. What was your average **annual** family income? _____ $

3. Multiply years x income to get lifetime income   (This is the amount of money you have made in your lifetime!)
   $_____

4. How much of that number do you have left in cash assets: (Don't count home equity just yet)
   $_____

Does your number make you want to vomit?

If you have been an excellent saver and your test number doesn't alarm you, I want to personally congratulate you on good habits and good choices. I hope you will continue your march toward a successful financial life for you and your family. Our country needs MORE people like YOU! If you haven't done a great job, welcome to the silent majority in the USA. Most people—despite making millions of dollars over a lifetime—are broke. In fact, 74% of the population that is past the age of sixty-five, lives below our nation's stated poverty line of $23,400. With the average Social Security check being about $1,320 per month, you sort of come to an understanding that saving money is very important for your own financial future.

We live in the USA, where we are blessed to have nearly-limitless opportunity. Yet, despite this great freedom, the statistics for the average working-American family is not so boastful. Consider this fact:

If we're making that kind of money that you showed in the equation above, why aren't we all millionaires yet?

WE MAKE MILLIONS DURING OUR LIFETIMES, BUT KEEP VERY LITTLE OF IT!

6 Reasons We Are Failing Financially:

1. __We Do Not Have A Savings Ethic__. I like the word ETHOS: From the British Dictionary: noun

*"the distinctive character, spirit,
and attitudes of a people, culture, era, etc"*

We are a spend-it-now, pay- for-it-later society. Instant gratification has pummeled most savings plans. Keeping up with the Jones'…. well, THE JONES' ARE BROKE TOO! (Sorry if your last name is Jones, I mean no disrespect here).

Also, we do not understand the power of time: Most people have great intentions and are hopeful, that 'AS SOON AS…" kicks in. As soon as:

…I get the kids out of school

…I get the debts paid off

…I get that next promotion

…I get that next degree

…I Find a better spouse

…I have more time

Here is what I have observed the last three decades as I have counseled people about money and lifestyle….

SOMEDAY NEVER COMES! The debt cycle, inflation, unplanned expenses and emergencies, the continual drain of everyday items like cell phones, computers, internet, and debts, not to mention the regular expenses for food, clothing, and shelter all seem to have moved the average family one step closer to financial ruin.

2. ***We do not understand how debt works***. These days it is so easy to get in to debt and so HARD to get out of it. There are certainly justifiable reasons for taking on a debt burden....health care costs, emergency costs, and other events where the acceptance of debt makes sense. However, most debt is NOT that kind of debt.

If you are in debt, it may require a very well executed plan to get out. So many people live in the debt trap, where their debt payments get so high, they may never get out of debt.

3. ***We overpay our taxes***. This is crazy. Seriously, stop this now. There is no favor shown to people who overpay a bill that simply is not due. Far too many people use these tax refunds to catch up. The very reason they may be behind is that they were over contributing to their tax bill in the first place. Crazy, huh?

I cannot find credible evidence anywhere that over paying your taxes just to get a refund back in April is a good financial move. It seems we all sit around in April, waiting for our tax refunds to show up. Talk about APRIL FOOLS!

4. ***Inflation is the invisible killer.***

Think about this.....let's say that you can live TODAY on $60,000 per year. Perhaps you are 35 years old with a goal of retiring at age 65. That is just 30 years from now, or 360 more paychecks before you are done.

If the inflation rate increases approximately 3% per year for the next 30 years, you will need approximately $145,000 per year then to pay for what $60,000 pays for today. See! $60,000 and $145,000 are the exact same number 30 years apart if inflation is just 3%.

Here is a quick historical example to illustrate this concept more clearly.

In 1984, the average wage was $16,135 per person. In just 30 short years, the average wage was $46,481. While quality of life and the savings rate did not go up, inflation brought both prices and incomes up by about 3.25% per year during that time.

$46,481 (2014) is about 3.5 times as much as $16,135 (1984).

$145,000 (2046) is only 2.25 times as much as $60,000! (2016).

This is actual historical data. You are gonna need more money later if inflation is present. Do YOU think prices may be going up? Do you have a plan to grow your retirement income during the retirement years?

What is happening right now? Not all incomes have kept up with inflation. Here is the good news! Inflation isn't your fault. It certainly has a massive impact on your well being, but you didn't cause it. Now, the fun part is to find out how to raise your income and lifestyle to meet the demands that inflation places on your well being.

Financially, it has been two steps forward and 2.1 steps backwards for many families. You will want to find investments that grow larger on average than the inflation rate. You will want to cut out debt and manage your money better knowing that inflation is the silent financial killer.

5. *Money things are confusing*. Many people bury their head in the sand, cross their fingers, play the lottery, and simply HOPE that things are going to work out. Here is something to know:

HOPE IS NOT A GOOD FINANCIAL PLAN

On top of that, there is so much information out in the world that it can get confusing! I get so many questions, and most of them are relevant questions…I hope you will keep asking! Here is a sample of the questions I have received in my office during the past month….

- Should I buy gold?
- Should I pay off my low interest tax deductible mortgage early?
- Hey Cash, I am broke and living on my mother's couch at the age of 50, what investments do you think I need?
- How do I start the right college savings plan for my kids?
- How do I afford a new house?
- How can I take care of myself and still give to my favorite charity?
- How do taxes work?
- Why are taxes so high?
- Is this all there is in life? Why is money so tough?
- Is it ever going to get better for me?
- How can a single mom take care of her kids, herself, and still plan for the future?
- Should I get a part time job or start a part time business? How does that work?
- Why is there so much month left at the end of the money?

And on and on it goes. These are all important questions, and here is something to know….there IS an answer to all of these questions! It just takes YOU to ask them to the right person, and to find the right information.

6. ***Family Culture.*** Perhaps all you have ever known is struggle. Many families pass down bad financial habits and these habits are soon cast upon the adult children. The cycle continues. My family was ALWAYS in debt. As a young man, I was ALWAYS in debt too. Why? I learned it. I duplicated my family methods.

I believe that copying off of your neighbor in life is actually a good idea. Is there someone you know that has what you want? Ask them questions. Copy. Now this is bad advice if you are in the third grade, but in life, copying successful behavior is something that will help you move forward financially.

You must be careful when taking advice from anyone. If you copy their advice, you might also copy their lifestyle. Perhaps your upbringing is your biggest stumbling block? If so, **take quick and massive action to learn what you can and implement wonderful, productive habits**.

The 7 things YOU Must Know To Become Wealthy
What Got You Here Won't Get You There!

These are behaviors that count. These are the common behaviors of the wealthy people that I have had the great fortune to work for and manage. These things can work for anybody. Would you be willing to make a few changes to improve?

Check out these seven things…they are simple!

1. **Do not go into "Bad Debt**

The average high interest credit card can take over 20 years to pay off. The borrower is a slave to the lender. Avoid long term, high-interest credit at all costs. Visa is not your friend. Many of these 0%

offerings escalate into 20% offerings if you don't adhere to the fine details. Instead, have 0% interest in debt. Be a saver.

2. **Do Not Over Pay Taxes**

According to the IRS, last year nearly 86% of the tax returns filed had a tax refund coming to them at an average rate of $3,100! This is simply crazy. Almost every family is overpaying their taxes. This is simply a bill that is not due and we are overpaying it. Are there other bills that are smart to over pay? Just one....your retirement bill!

3. **Invest For The Long Term**

Invest well. Find a method that suits you for investing. This could be your ticket to the life you want. Make sure you understand risks and all of the elements of investing before investing a single cent. Get educated on investing, or hire someone who meets your criteria. Examine the 401k at work, the Roth IRA, and other strategies to make sure you are on the right track.

Once you decide to invest, make a commitment to yourself NOT to spend these long term dollars on short term items. You will thank me later.

4. **Minimize Risk**

The years 2000, 2001, 2002, 2008, 2009 taught us a lesson. If the market falls 30% again, it will require a 43% gain just to break even! Losing money in the market, even though expected sometimes, can be devastating. Talk to your investment people about their strategy for down markets.

Of course, there are many kinds of risk to manage....inflation is a risk , taxes are a huge risk , adult kids who drain your bank accounts can be a risk, and procrastination is risk as well!

5. __Have a Long Term Vision With Short-Term Behavior__

Don't buy shoes or dinner with your retirement account money. Enough said. Behavior counts and will reward you or incriminate you as you grow.

6. __Be Liquid. Be Cash Wealthy__

Contemplate the habits that got you here. Have liquid savings so you aren't ever tempted to go in to debt. Get this right. Cash is King. (I like the way that sounds!) Most people go in debt because they have skipped this part. Accumulate a large emergency/expense fund. Sell things you don't need. Don't buy frivolous stuff. Remember, The Joneses' are broke.

7. __Don't Interrupt Compounding__

Putting investment money in, then taking it out for vacation, then putting it back in, then taking it out again…this is crazy! Investments ARE NOT "put and take accounts". Time is your friend and you will want to invest and give the money a chance to grow and compound over time. Don't sacrifice your long term well being for your short term desires. It isn't worth it.

Have 80 year old you talk to 40 year old you and imagine what you might say to yourself if this were possible!!! The older version of you is always the wisest!!!

Chapter 3:
Do Numbers Make You NUMB?

I hear these things all the time.....

- I am not a numbers person

- Math is not my strong point

- My spouse "takes care" of everything

- I am going to win the lottery, none of this stuff matters

- The politicians are gonna mess it up anyway, why should I care?

- I don't want to be a millionaire; I just want to be comfortable...

To this I say, "Baloney! Hogwash! Blah Blah Blah!" While some of these statements may have some merit, **none** of them is actually true or going to help you have what you want and need.

Even the least number oriented person still has to pay bills, and medical care, and gasoline. Numbers are everywhere. You ARE a numbers person, you just don't realize it! I bet if your employer shorted you on your paycheck, you would figure it out! If your eight year-old wanted a $250 pair of Nike Air Jordan shoes, you would be enough of a numbers person to deal with that also! I believe that once the veil of secrecy is taken away from the money game, the more confident you will actually be. Taking action helps. I call it ***ACE... ACTION CURES EVERYTHING***!

Math doesn't have to be your strong point....you can delegate math to someone else...it is your dreams and goals that need to be your strong point! I have not met many people who don't have particular dreams and goals. What I HAVE learned is that almost every goal and dream has some price tag associated with it.

Your life is YOUR responsibility. At some point, the scoreboard lights up and represents how well you did in the game of life/ money. Perhaps some event will allow you to ignore money forever, but in my experience, everyone will want to be accountable...TO THEMSELVES!

Once you have the basics, the numbers begin to make more sense. Little by little, you can learn the basics. <u>Oh yea, you will want to write this down....</u>

> # To Survive Retirement, YOU Absolutely MUST Become A Millionaire!

Here is a simple formula that you will enjoy following. I call it the ***"Income Drawdown Formula"***. Let's make one assumption, that during retirement you will have a stash of money somewhere, and you want to take money FROM these investments to live on.

Researchers tell us that we can exhaust these savings at a rate of between 3-6% per year depending on our age, so let's use the number 5% as our "drawdown number". If you have $1,000,000 in your savings and decide to liquidate 5% per year for retirement, it would spit out exactly $50,000. Guess what, to live at a median income of $50,000 per year from your investments requires that you have $1,000,000 somewhere! You MUST become a millionaire. Almost all of us have had over a million dollars come through our hands by the end of life.....where is it?

Chapter 4:
Family Habits: Behavior Matters. Oh, And Your Kids Are Watching

Wouldn't it be great to know that our kids were all going to be ok financially? Unfortunately for me, I spent the first 18 years of my life training with my parents on how to be broke and miserable. It just seemed like financial ugly was my destiny.

How many times do our kids hear the word "NO" by the time they are 18? Lots! I was conditioned for failure. Have YOU used any of these phrases?

- Money doesn't grow on trees
- Put it back, too expensive
- We can't afford that
- If you make too much money you go to…….
- The rich get richer, the poor get poorer
- Don't get your hopes up son…(one of my favorites)
- Don't put all your eggs in one basket
- Get a degree, get a good job, everything will be fine
- The secret to success is to go to college

My responses to the endless line of baloney fed to me by society over my lifetime:

Money does grow on trees….Family Trees

It wasn't too expensive....I was too poor

We couldn't afford this thing but we made a provision for cigarettes...maybe it was just a scam to keep me from getting what I needed

If you make too much money, you become more of what you already are...if you are already a jerk, you become jerkier....If you are a good and decent human, more money allows you to help more people, build more churches, help more hungry, build more schools, and help people around the world do better. Money is not the root of all evil, the Love of money is. I don't love money. I do love what it can do to better the lives of mankind.

The rich do get richer. They know stuff. I helped them get rich. This book is a starting point for you to get richer too. The rich also **wanted** to get richer. Do you?

Do get your hopes up. Very up. It takes more energy to be negative than positive. Have huge, audacious, big, hairy goals and then go figure out how to accomplish them. Better to aim for the stars and miss by half than aim for nothing then become that.

Eggs in one basket? Who comes up with this stuff? Ray Kroc (McDonalds) Sam Walton (WalMart) Bill Gates (Microsoft) and others put all of their eggs in one basic basket, then took the right steps with those eggs and all of the sudden had more eggs than you could ever fit into all the baskets in the world. Take care of your eggs. And your basket!

Get a degree? I believe that the number one new debt is college loans. They come in all age categories too. These debts are lasting lifetimes for people. Stay out of debt. Make sure it is worth it. The world is changing. Consider all of your options. Perhaps a college degree is the way to success, but for many of my millionaire clients it had almost nothing to do with it.

The idea that a college degree is a free ticket to success is perhaps one of the biggest misconceptions today. People are running up college debt at alarming rates. The job market and how we make a living these days has changed too, and relying on the idea of the guaranteed job at the end of college is something that can be relied on is nothing more than a fantasy.

I have a college degree. I am a bit ashamed at the money I spent getting it. My diploma is in a drawer in my garage. Not one person has ever asked me about it. Perhaps my life might have been better to have had the $100,000 expense show up in my savings account at the beginning of my life, rather than on my credit report for the 15 years that followed.

Don't confuse wives tales and nursery rhymes as truth. Money is a tool. How it works is a science. How you do with it is 100% on you. The government isn't going to help you be happy or get what you want. That is your quest!

Chapter 5:
Getting Started NOW Is So Easy.
Feel better today!
MINDSET---DESIRE---ACTION

RIGHT NOW THIS VERY MINUTE, GO FIND ONE DOLLAR.
SERIOUSLY, GO GET A BUCK!

This is your starting point. Take a picture of it. Do a dollar selfie! This dollar is symbolic for you. It represents a starting line. Sort of like those first steps you took as an infant. Take that dollar and put it in a jar and put it in a place where you can see it every day. Put it in a jar perhaps with a label that you can write on. On that label, write a number that you believe you can achieve over the next few years.

Protect this dollar. **NEVER SPEND IT FOR ANYTHING**. Make a pledge to your future that **THIS** dollar is special, in that it will save you when you are older. It is your port in a storm. It is your shelter. This is the dollar where it all went right. Now, you have done it! Step one accomplished.

Ok, I know some of you want to read to the end. Go put your buck away before you read any more. Seriously, you will be amazed by how good it feels to take this one, simple, life affirming step.

Step two: Repeat step one at every opportunity. NEVER SPEND THIS MONEY. Commit right now. **Great things are about to happen**.

With a positive money mindset, you will now begin to recognize opportunities to save for your future. We aren't going to use this money to pay debts, buy stuff right now, take care of the kids, or anything else to take care of YOU!

This is the very first step to getting to wealth…mindset….desire…. then action. You just took action. My assumption is that you WANT to be well off.

Right now feel accomplished. You took a step. Would you be willing to email me a selfie with your dollar? Seriously…I need to be encouraged too…AND, I will put it on our blog site to show the world!!!! cash@solomonway.com

Chapter 6:
Safeguarding Your Family: There ARE Monsters Under The Bed!

Ok, listen up. No one likes this part. We will get through it quickly. There are some things you MUST know. They are yucky. Let's get to a point where you know that you know that you know that you stepped up and took care of business in advance.

Right now the death rate in the USA is hovering right at 100%. (Did I just make you laugh at death? I hope so!) Make a plan, especially if you have a spouse or kids.

Here are the rules of survival:

- ***Buy the right amount of life insurance for yourself so your spouse and kids are ok, even if you aren't***. You will need about 20 times your income to leave the right amount for your kids....so if you make $50,000 per year, find a suitable policy for $1,000,000. Your family could take out $50,000 per year from the policy and be ok financially for quite some time.

- ***Get a will***. This process is so simple. Get a power of attorney for medical stuff and directives to physicians. These are all simple to accomplish. If you don't know how to do it, ask your advisor for help. Email me; I can help point you in the right direction. Do not miss this step. Way too many people think they are invincible. Don't be that person. GO FUND ME is **NOT** a will!

- **_Protect your identity_**. There are some really popular companies who do this and there are some really good ones who do this for you. Seriously, your identity is a big deal. What would you do if someone stole your name and committed a crime as you or got healthcare as you?

These are the three biggies that haunt families. These are **irreversible mistakes**. Fix this while you can. You will find massive relief once this is accomplished....I am proud of you....take this step.

Chapter 7:
Getting Out Of Debt: G.O.O.D.
(AND HOW TO STAY OUT OF DEBT FOREVER!)

Ever heard any these?

- The borrower is a slave to the lender

- The rich rule over the poor

- I owe, I owe, so it's off to work I go!

Is it possible that you have actually used some of these words yourself? Wouldn't it be nice to eliminate this vocabulary from your brain?

I have heard them all. **<u>Debt is the number one destroyer of dreams</u>** and lifestyle in the modern era. It is an epidemic. It is calculated to work against families.

What is a financial debt? ANYTHING YOU OWE SOMEONE ELSE.

Do you have these kinds of debts?

- Credit Cards

- Taxes

- Property taxes

- Medical Bills

- Mortgages

- Loans
- Same As Cash deals
- Family Loans

There are probably more...these will do for now...

Why do we need to get out of bad debt? Here is what I have experienced:

1. You feel awful while in debt and wonderful when out of debt
2. You lose time with your money as you allocate it to the debt, not growth
3. Compound interest works for you or against you.

Would you like to be out of debt forever? If right this moment you could snap your fingers and magically be out of debt, how would you feel immediately after that?

Here is the first step to getting out of debt and staying out of debt forever:

1. Right now this exact moment make a declaration to yourself... A decision that you will never go back on...decide to get and **stay out of debt**. Too many people think debt is okay as a lifestyle and I could NOT DISAGREE MORE. DEBT is not a lifestyle. It is bondage. It is fear. It is lost opportunity. **Debt is a LIE**! It is NOT the way to financial freedom.

2. The second step is to begin to save assets so that you never have to go back into debt. No more BONDAGE. NO MORE FINANCIAL SLAVERY. Seriously, this step is so important and most miss it. They get focused on easing the pain that they never step into the moment where they eliminate the cause of the pain. It

is like taking a painkiller for a fractured arm. At some point, you have to fix what is broken. <u>This step assures you a better chance at financial freedom</u>.

There are multiple ways to structure debt reduction. Once again I believe the first step is to create a valid savings program so that we cure the cause, not the pain of debt. A professional advisor can help you create the right kind of repayment program. There may be a season for you and your family where you have to make sacrifices to get debt paid off. And I encourage you to welcome and enjoy the season of what may be your most profitable endeavor!

When you are debt free, I am going to ask you a favor: I want you to email me and have a conversation about how good it feels to get out of debt. Fair enough?

Email Me Here: ***debtfree@solomonway.com***

Congratulations on making a decision....this is gonna be GREAT for you!

Chapter 8:
Quick Guide For The Self Employed

One of my favorite phrases is "The American Dream." I would be curious to know your definition of the American Dream. Mine would include something like being my own boss, controlling my own destiny, and being in complete control of my success or failure. There are many kinds of self-employment and with each of them there are many things to know.

After counseling with hundreds of small business owners, I have compiled a list of things you will want to master or understand as you move through the world of self-employment and towards the American Dream. Most of these have to do with the simple question, "How Do I Run My Business?"

Regardless of the size or scope of your business, the following items will get you on the right path toward success.

1. <u>Get separate checking accounts</u>. Never co-mingle work money and personal money . I see this as one of the biggest mistakes made by the self-employed. If you can find a way to run your business from just one checking/debit account you will be on your way to a well run and successful business.

2. <u>Choose the right corporate entity.</u> You may choose to be a sole proprietor, C Corporation, or a LLC Corporation. While there are

other forms of business ownership, these three seem to comprise the majority of small business in America today.

I feel like a sole proprietorship position is perhaps the most dangerous, given that it usually taxed at the highest level. Consult with your tax and financial professional to understand the differences between LLCs, corporations, and a sole proprietorship.

Each entity type may also provide certain levels of asset protection. These are all questions best answered by your CPA/Advisor/Attorney. Make sure you do not just assume that you are doing it the best way for your business. Ask questions. Get answers. Be certain!

3. <u>Stay on top of your bookkeeping</u>. One of the most frustrating times of the year is April when everyone is running around trying to remember what they did a year ago and how to report it to the tax guy. Daily or weekly wrap-up meetings for yourself will help keep your business on track 365 days a year. Consider delegating all of your bookkeeping if it is not your strength. You will also want to keep a separate written log for all the miles you drive.

4. <u>Leverage the power of social media</u>. I believe that things like Facebook and Twitter can be beneficial to your small business if used in the right proportions. Nobody likes the guy who is constantly pitching his business. In fact I have seen people be successful on Facebook by posting 70% about themselves and their family and posting no more than 30% about their business. Be mindful of what <u>you</u> like on Facebook and put that same type of material out there.

5. <u>Network. Make an effort to meet and greet new people.</u> Prospect for new potential clients. Now make sure you realize that

networking and not working are spelled almost the same. As you grow your business it is vital to your continued success to meet new people with similar interests. If you aren't great at presenting or public speaking, join a class like Toastmasters to improve your skills.

Master your elevator pitch. When somebody asks what you do you need to have a response prepared that is automatic and genuine. People make a decision about you in the first 15 seconds they know you. Make those 15 seconds count and master how you introduce yourself to people.

Collaborating with non competitive people from other industries is an excellent way to increase awareness of your business. For example, if you are a mortgage person, you may want to have a circle of realtors, financial advisors, CPA's, lawyers, construction people, maintenance people and more to go to when one of your clients needs a particular kind of help. Being "in the know" will serve your existing clients and may very well bring new client relationships right to your door.

6. Consider working with a success coach. A good coach can provide valuable insight that is usually hidden from you! SELF EVALUATION is actually a rare thing. The truly great athletes all have coaches. Why not you? Ultimately, a great coach makes you way more money than they cost you. Something else to consider: Tiger Woods has a coach. Michael Jordan has a coach. Almost every successful athlete has a coach that they give thanks to. Having an extra set of eyes is invaluable. Why not you?

At a minimum, ask someone you trust to listen to you as you present your biz to other people. Don't be afraid of criticism, seek it. It will help you win.

7. <u>Stay on top of your taxes</u>. Just like bookkeeping, stay on top of your taxes. One of the biggest hurdles is to stay up to date on your taxes. Consider making a separate account for taxes. You will owe the self-employment tax (approximately 15% of your profits) PLUS the income tax. Also, sales taxes are critical for you to keep up to date.

Keep track of miles, meals, and any expenses incurred on behalf of your business. If you travel, there are different rules for writing off those expenses. A close relationship with a tax person is a GREAT idea!

8. <u>Reward yourself</u>. Success does not come cheap. Set meaningful goals that can be rewarded with a nice dinner or a trip.

9. <u>Success requires these three elements:</u>

URGENCY

CONSISTENCY

TIME

Many people are consistent, but aren't urgent. Some are urgent, but only for a moment. Some are just all over the map. To win in business requires these three things to operate at the same time, all the time.

10. <u>Know your numbers</u>. Seriously, we talked about this before. You must know how profits work. You must know how many sales to break even and to profit.

- How many sales to make a profit
- How many presentations to make a sale
- How many approaches/calls to set a kept appointment

- How much are my bills

- How much are my taxes

- How much are my supplies and other related expenses

- How much is my own time worth? One of the most important numbers. Should you be doing $12 an hour work rather than doing $200 per hour sales work? Consider the true cost/value to an assistant.

Knowing the numbers of your business is vital. If you simply cannot operate the numbers, then find a credible person who can do all the numbers for you.

11. Be Bold. The universe does not reward sissies. Your belief in yourself and your business should be sky high. If you don't believe in yourself, no one else will either.

There are many other things that will be required from you. These are the basics and must be mastered immediately. If there is something on this list you simply cannot do then get help before moving forward.

Chapter 9:
Take The Next Step. Now or never!

Remember that part in the Indiana Jones Movie where he had to take a step across a cavern at a place where there was nothing but a 200 foot drop into a death filled cavern? Whew, that one sticks with me. Business is much like that. Sometimes we have to step where there is no step. Much will be required from you. The rewards will be worth it.

I will finish with just a few things here that I consider to be key elements to having a successful business life in the pursuit of the American Dream.

1. Be careful to whose opinion you listen. When you buy somebody's opinion you may also by their lifestyle and outcome! Your friends may not really have your best interest in mind and rarely know what you're going through. If they do not know your goal set or motivation, why would you put a value on what someone else thinks?

Often, in business, you must be willing to endure a temporary loss of social esteem from ignorant people. Toughen up. Lions never lose sleep over the opinions of sheep. You will need a backbone, not a WISHbone.

2. Set a schedule. Know when you are going to work. Keep a calendar. Be on time, be prompt. Lead by example. Be awesome!

3. How you do ANYTHING is how you do EVERYTHING. Have a culture of excellence. Beat your competition with excellence. Have a standard so high that no one else can understand it.

The book of Proverbs states, "Show me a man skilled in his work and he will serve before Kings and Queens, and not obscure men." The idea of excellence is universal. But excellence is rare. So is success. They go together.

4. Invest in personal and self development. There are so many great teachers out there. Check YouTube and get out there and learn more and more about yourself and your craft. Self development is a lifetime idea. It is sort of like bathing...you need to do it every day for it to be most effective! Seminars, CDs , Webinars, Classes, Continuing Education....all of these are designed to help you.

Drive Time University: Turn off your talk radio. It just makes you hate the world and everything in it. Invest in your brain. Invest in your heart. Invest in your intellect and vocabulary. If you are in your car, listen to something that makes you better by the time your journey ends. If you could get just 2% better at something each week, you can be 100% better within a year. And what would it be like if your income increased 100%?

5. Understand the season of life you are in. It is going to take time, consistency, urgency, and sacrifice. Here is one of THE BIGGEST TOPICS I HAVE HAD TO OVERCOME IN RUNNING A BUSINESS:

How do I build this business and not neglect my kids and family?

This is a tough one especially for me. How do you keep your life in balance while sitting out on this journey?

From a practical standpoint, keeping calendar and scheduling time with my family helps ease my burden. However, there were periods in my life that required great sacrifice. Much sacrifice will be expected from you as well. All I can tell you is that it is worth it. The sacrifice is for the benefit of your family.

- At one point in my life my children were my excuse NOT to go big. Now they are my reason WHY TO go big. They understand I'm trying to build something magnificent and I believe the juice is worth the squeeze. I am willing to pay a little cost now to have a big reward later. They will learn much more from an attempt than an excuse. Your kids are watching.

- Kids are more durable than we think. Your kids are watching.

- I do not pay attention to my friend's opinions of how I raise my family. This is my shot, my turn, and I will raise them exactly as I please. My kids are watching me and learning some of the greatest lessons in life. To learn the value of sacrifice and dedication at an early age will benefit them all of their lives. Your kids are watching.

- We were never promised an easy life. Comfort is the enemy of achievement. I am the provider for my family and I will do what it takes, for however long it takes to get the job done. Imagine how it will feel when you AND your family are sitting on a luxurious beach, sipping age-appropriate drinks from a pineapple and living the good life while all of the doubters, naysayers, and haters are sitting on a highway, waiting to get to a JOB (Just Over Broke) that they do not love and that does not REALLY take care of their most intimate dreams and goals. Your kids are watching.

- What are you willing to fight for? Life gives you what you are willing to fight for, not what you want, or what you deserve, or what you claim….it takes work, consistency, and the occasional karate kick to the pants. Your kids are watching.

- Remember when you were dating that special someone? Remember how dedicated you were and how much you thought about each other and how it was all you think about? Treat your business this same way and you will reap wonderful rewards! Your kids are watching.

- Involve your kids. Let them know the goals. I told my kids recently, *"Girls, daddy is gonna be in the trenches for about 90 days while I go for this goal of ours. Do I have your permission to go for it and win big for our family? At the end of this goal period, how about I take some of our profits and take a fun trip to Disney World and Epcot Center? May I have your permission?"*

Now, my children are my accountability partners! When I come in from a long day, I hear, "Daddy, did you get any new clients today? Daddy, how was work…" At this point they are angry when I come home early since they know Disney waits with each new success! Once I allowed myself to be successful FOR my kids instead using my kids as an excuse, the game changed.

Ultimately, I will never do anything to harm my kids and my spouse. They are my reason for working towards excellence. They inspire me. I believe my work and commitment will inspire them as well.

WRAP UP

I want to congratulate you on taking a step. Time is short. It really is time to get started. This book is designed to help you ask lots of important questions and get them answered. The ideas here can speed up your success and help you avoid common mistakes in life.

You can be successful with money and business. ANYBODY can. God does not make any junk. Perhaps you have failed before, and hopefully, you have learned so many valuable lessons to make the next attempt better. That is how life works. Plan...DO....Review!

So, are you ready to get started? Let's go create some new habits. Let's strengthen some excellent beliefs. Let's all go kick mediocrity to the curb and show the world how it is done. You need this. We need this. Your kids need this. Your community needs this.

We don't need a better President. We need better citizens who are debt free and productive. The time to take action is now.

This is YOUR SEASON.

GAME ON!

AFTERWARD

Are you really ready to get started? Did this book move you? Many people came to me after the first publication and said, "Wow, Cash, I am ready to get started, what do I do?"

So, for those of you who are ready to take whatever next step is appropriate for you, here are some simple suggestions on how to move forward.

- Find a Money University class near you and participate....these are FREE classes and will help you immensely! Email us at *info@solomonway.com* to get a listing of our next classes

- Read a book with practical application knowledge. You will want to implement changes at some point.

- Stay informed! Join our mailing list at info@solomonway.com by simply sending us a request! We will occasionally send an article or invite to something financially related that can benefit you!

Cash Matthews

www.solomonway.com

www.moneyuniversitythebook.com

cash@solomonway.com